snow b...

Yukiko Kido

flip-a

WORD

Word Families

The world is full of print. Written words are everywhere. It's impossible to learn printed words by memorizing them word, by word, by word. To make learning easier, words can be grouped into families.

The words in a word family have two or more letters that are the same. We read "ate" words and "eet" words, "it" words and "ow" words. If you know "eet," then it's easier to learn beet, feet, and street.

This book has words from three different word families. All the words in a family rhyme—which means you can add other words to the group by changing the first letter.

It's okay if some of the words you think of are not *real* words. If you make "geet" or "keet" or "reet," it's not wrong— as long as you know the difference between a real word and a nonsense word.

Flip each page and presto-change-o— a new word appears!

The

Family

c
n
k
m
g
p
h
r
d
s
w

beet

street

beet on feet

feet meet

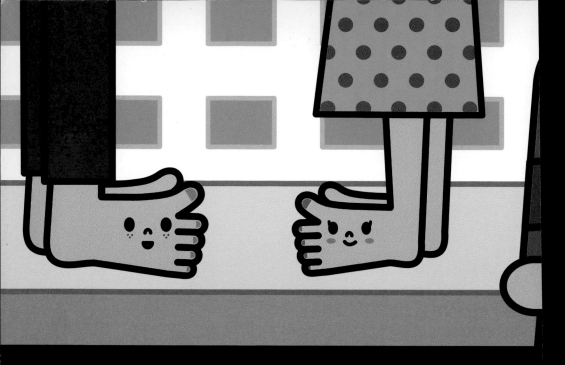

feet meet on the street

beet on the street

The

Family

f
l
w
m
g
n
b
r
d
w
t

crate

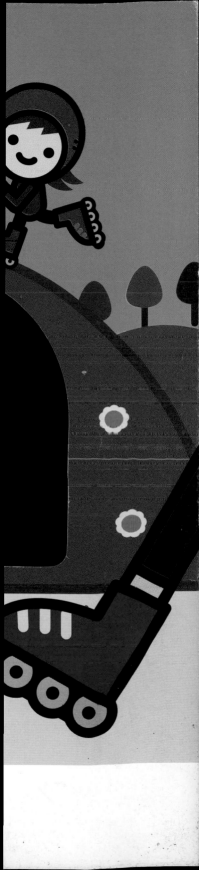

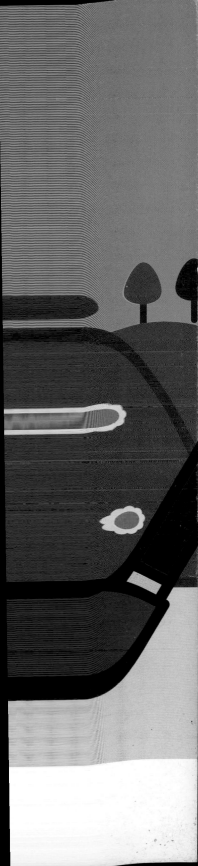

plate

skate through a gate

skate on a plate

skate in a crate

plate in a crate

The

Family

f
l
w
m
g
n
b
r
d
w
t

row

t h r

b o w

snow bow

row in snow

throw snow

throw bow

The eet Family

beet	meet
feet	sheet
greet	street

The ate Family

crate	hate
date	plate
fate	rate
gate	skate

The ow Family

bow	row
crow	show
grow	snow
mow	throw

Find the words in each family.